Pig State Love Songs
© Ben Ptolemy 2016
All Rights Reserved.

ISBN# 978-0-9908957-2-5

" in the traditional non-traditional way "

25-14-21-9-31 — 31-9-21-14-25

Imagician Press
Greensboro, North Carolina
The United States of America

Cover: *FrankenJesus Before Pilate,* oil on canvas by Alvin Ward
Graphic design by Sonji Noodles

PIG STATE
LOVE SONGS

PIG STATE
LOVE SONGS

—for
Charles and Weronika

PIG STATE
LOVE SONGS

Ben Ptolemy

Ben Ptolemy

Pig State Love Songs

< >

sitting in a booth with eyes closed
—not dead
just ketchup

< >

the ant in the salt shaker
reminding me
frugality

Two

< >

depths of the oceans
mountain tops also
the boundaries of the fiend

< >

beginning the exile
a fire on the first try
still too cold to smile

< >

how far will one get
hiding the obvious
the onions eaten in secret

Pig State Love Songs

< >

dusk til dawn curfews
considering my ways
o moon please peek for me

< >

the edges of outer space
underground
the boundaries of the fiend

< >

at the end of the day
what it may mean to another
—scrounging

Four

< >

a surface reality
if there is ever proof
cameras in use

< >

more fun than you will ever admit to
good times!
—in asterisk city

< >

razzle-dazzle
glitters from a distance
gazing for a companion

Pig State Love Songs

< >

"a year and a day without..."
the message left at the tone
stranded.

< >

where the world feels like Saturday
in these woods
the last Tuesday of Spring

< >

In April's cold rain
the pine trees sway
green with company

Six

< >

last night wearing the camouflaged shirt
but she could still tell
i was drunk

< >

surrounded by spies
when you whisper
the moral of the story

< >

at the bar
where i said i wouldn't be—
happy

Pig State Love Songs

< >

what's to explain
a glance at the plow
And the clouds...

< >

sure, this is mission control
secret mission boy
BUT where are you now?

< >

floating from the peak
weather which took a leap
overcoming the ruts—

Eight

< >

you wanna move
but what's the use
sundown in a can of the blues

< >

one more sip
then to escape
no-pressure land

< >

pretend you have the option
 and still don't want to
—restricted

Pig State Love Songs

< >

pretend you have the option
 and still don't want to
—unaddicted

< >

i didn't laugh
thinking to myself
"lol"

Ten

< >

yo, back off homey!
cruising through a ghetto
at 90 b.p.m.

< >

in between warehouses
on the outskirts
distant dreams

< >

saw the officer
parked on the street
was he also writing poetry?

Pig State Love Songs

< >

past seven years
in the city
ain't nothing but a change of slang—

< >

in chicken village
used car dealers and sidewalks
lost in thought

< >

in chicken village
chickenscratch
at the traffic light

Twelve

< >

in chicken village
old man, mountain bike
riding it like it's stolen

< >

in chicken village
the beginning of Summer
brother, i'm talking *fried!*

< >

in chicken village
styrofoam glows
this is a journey

Pig State Love Songs

< >

in chicken village
—a pig!
in each parking lot

< >

in chicken village
you gotta cross to the other side
for roast beef

< >

robbed!
in front of everybody
two dollars for a chicken leg...

Fourteen

< >

in chicken village
c s i
talkin' about bigger fish to fry

< >

in chicken village
you're better off
going cold turkey

Pig State Love Songs

< >

in a world
behind the surface world
the quota continues

< >

resting on a porchswing
mosquitoes
always hungry

< >

on the day after quitting
a discount
from the piper

Sixteen

< >

out of place here
in the meat market
heart on a sleeve

< >

like all the others
catching a buzz
the bartender spies another fly

< >

drinking 'round the rich
drinking 'round the poor
the same generosity

Pig State Love Songs

< >

no distractions
by a wall of glass
clouds that look like clouds

< >

despite how shapes may appear
from the outside
this is my lucky life

< >

—got a few allies
ok waiting 'til later
which won't ask why

Eighteen

< >

a kiss on the cheek
—just a kiss on the cheek
ah, your wife is nice

< >

clouds in battle
above the city
weathermen agree it's an iffy

< >

clouds in battle
city by city
these *internacionale bragging rights*

Pig State Love Songs

< >

bouncing around
like her tits are special
that girl with a fine, fine ass

< >

manned stools fanned in unison
turning in a wave
when she walks by

< >

a kiss on the cheek
—just a kiss on the cheek
ah, can't think thrice

Twenty

⟨ ⟩

entering bar blinds
sudden bright light!
and even the dead drunks go aaahhhhh!

⟨ ⟩

wing bones
swimming in the sauce
—but it's a secret!

⟨ ⟩

the waitress
with such a sweet face
giving me a go-to-hell look

Pig State Love Songs

< >

whisker gray
scratching the surface
maybe all of it *was* a mistake

< >

Sonji when, at last, you return
remember
the earth *is* a moody place

< >

illumination
a let down
the dose at the bottom of the well

Twenty Two

< >

what's to explain
another tug on the chain
metamorphosis hurts

< >

not a matter of perception.
half-way through the other side
—broken

Pig State Love Songs

< >

some days good
some days, oh well
if you want consistent check the worry

< >

tick and tock
nudging the night on
echoes winding down a hall

< >

middle of the night glow
reheating leftovers
dragon on a to-go carton

Twenty Four

< >

hollow suburbia
skylines in droop
the sinking crescent moon

< >

together again
more like old friends, unspeaking
booze and the excuse

< >

undecided as yet...
luck versus the curfew
i think of her *i do*

Pig State Love Songs

< >

sloppy Joe's
dreaming eyes closed
never enough info

< >

somewhere else better to be
rain crashes on the hood
a passing taxi

Twenty Six

< >

world news on the radio
useless data
the hermit goes to town

< >

what's wrong?
it's just beer and pizza
sometimes i think you're no damn fun

< >

one Carolina, two Carolina:
hide 'n seek
with the police

Pig State Love Songs

< >

treading delicately
on the holiday
blue lights on the prowl

< >

lurking deputies
don't think we don't know
a classic fear of bridges

< >

glancing back again
reoccuring rear view blues
things that have to pass?

Twenty Eight

< >

poetry worth remembering
approaching the traffic light
as it turns green

< >

it's changing make a choice!
given all these roads
no longer leading home

< >

signs… fade
birds… sing in the rain
it don't take a genius to catch a train

Pig State Love Songs

< >

why you've been driving around
like an idiot
the phone just don't know

< >

at pilgrimage's end
woo-hoo
the pleasures so pursued

< >

surrounded
such beautiful distractions
the life not yet over

Thirty

< >

poorboy
that atlas of forbidden things
—what the cute waitress brings

< >

had my fingers crossed
activating plans
with the money i owe you

< >

(what they hear)
(not what was meant at all)
(the invisible beer can wall)

Pig State Love Songs

< >

(what they heard)
(not what was said at all)
(the invisible beer can wall)

< >

front row seats!
thy sweet polished mahogany...
don't talk

< >

laughing at the entire world
myself—too
training for the next haiku

Thirty Two

< >

all day long without a guilty thought
hooky
in paradise

< >

10,000 missed opportunities
quitting the day job
to follow the dream

< >

such a crazy night
—but she knows
sneaking a peek at the one i like

Pig State Love Songs

< >

ignoring a menu
sipping a brew
feeling good about these chances

< >

inebriatedly
compiling the memoir
how i quit drinking

< >

lingering over the half-pint
a wee-bit tipsy
O Henry...

Thirty Four

< >

the overcast Friday
dusks of Summer
sidekick buy i another

< >

in the bar closest to your house
on every side
an empty seat

< >

thinking of her
a sigh resumes
no way to get a message too

Pig State Love Songs

< >

massive cloudscapes
miles and miles of airtime
antenna towers scrawny

< >

by request
a farewell is all that's left
breathlessly inspired

< >

dear police state
imagine it *Your Way*
—from your secret admirer

Ben Ptolemy

Ben Ptolemy

Pig State Love Songs

interrogated!
i've overcome everything
  but my next desire

< >

ain't worried about not worrying
taking a chance
on plan A

Forty

< >

thin after the rent
even the sandwich
still making it why worry

< >

might as well smile
hey, old baloney
here comes another Monday

< >

the grasp—
isolation's diet
what falls out when you open the fridge

Pig State Love Songs

< >

three days in a row.
under pressure.
whatever makes *them* happy

< >

two days in a row
—almost
the sound of the can goes psssshhht!

< >

even if you might be right
—be nice
don't throw spaghetti

< >

washing dishes, clothes
as the grudge grows
a month since i've been kissed

< >

wallerin' around
the way of pigs.
rainy day time-management

< >

drunk and still drinking
before sunset
yes, depressed

Pig State Love Songs

< >

after the rain
it rained some more
hound with its chin on the floor

< >

memories of the bar
sloppily devoured
Mr. White shirt liked those ribs…

< >

stuck at home
yesterday's clone
no postage necessary

Forty Four

< >

thinking of the porch that needs sweeping
yep
thinking about it

< >

weeds swaying weeds bent
sunset's on the fence
the anti-social schedule.

< >

giving my regards to the chef
meatballs 'n spaghetti
with an easy pull-lid

Pig State Love Songs

< >

side street distractions
running out of cash
as the weekend begins

< >

complimentary
tickets for a game
the good times missed

< >

sitting in a swivel chair
to stay or to go
decisions, decisions

Forty Six

‹ ›

almost success
in a free man's land
stumbling over excuses

‹ ›

so you risked nothing
good for you
said the competition

‹ ›

inspirationless
crock-pot shifts
you don't know the half of it

Pig State Love Songs

< >

the vibe for today
could go either way
lots of raindrops on a speedbump

< >

it only takes belief
Sonji, don't be weak
levitating over the hump

< >

anything, something—
let's celebrate!
party supplies for a normal day

Forty Eight

< >

unavailable at the convenience store
—patience please
on market street

< >

vultures converge and hop
crossing the street
an old truck rusts in the weeds

< >

a rearrangement of internal things
blame the extremes
what else could it be?

Pig State Love Songs

< >

isolatable
catching a lift
spare parts

< >

a shed snake's skin
noticed a hermit
passing through the back yard

< >

hottest day of the year
basking in the shade
how sweet the breeze

< >

in chicken village
these pre-heated streets
could be 100 degrees

< >

in chicken village
noon-hour traffic
at twenty after six

Pig State Love Songs

< >

in chicken village
chicken in a box
on a nickname basis

< >

in chicken village
in between puffs of clouds
unfinished bid'ness

< >

in chicken village
old man, ten-speed bike
riding it like it's stolen

Fifty Two

< >

in chicken village
the sky falls every night
who gives a cluck, right?

< >

in chicken village
bums cuss
cats hiss

< >

in chicken village
there's lines around the block
there's foul language

Pig State Love Songs

< >

on the way home
talking on the phone
chicken in a bucket

< >

in chicken village
a u-turn swerve
that's a good deal, *bitch*

Fifty Four

< >

in chicken village
stomach blames brain
lured by an ad campaign

< >

in chicken village
watch out!
the over-flowing parking lot says delicious

< >

a last minute conviction
turning 90 degrees
hubcap goes free

Pig State Love Songs

< >

going down the sidewalk
damn hot sunny day
thy doppelganger looks grumpy

< >

distance yawns
both sides of the road
searching for the exile companion

< >

rain flat.
on the glossy street
the last of the bright fallen leaves

< >

lethargic hopes
boarded-up businesses
billboards for the lottery

< >

six straight days of rain in a row
come on
lucky number seven

< >

it's the graffiti of poverty
look out crackers
spray can cheese

Pig State Love Songs

< >

pig state strategies
luck versus the curfew...
some for later too?

< >

rolling out of the 'hood
—just a plate lunch portion
with the munchies

< >

badge state paranoia
such bullshsssz!
why the pig on the billboard grins

.

< >

crinkle fries you presume
in a parking lot
—area under surveillance—

< >

moonlight
on the municipal reservoir
who do you think you are?

< >

it's only natural
exploring boundaries
the fallen pine squishing a fence

Pig State Love Songs

< >

bright cold sunny day
tourists on the highway
unmarked cars

< >

ah, life
going down the road less-travelled
the occasional accident

< >

a tale of Whoa!
they come, they go
militant Highway Patrol

Sixty

< >

getting back
just the thought alone hurts
homeless beanstalk giant

< >

wrong side of town
sitting atop the world
mere coincidence?

Pig State Love Songs

< >

side by side on main
in the pouring rain
whispering names of angels

< >

that type of day
bar beer screen game
yawning at the score

< >

upon a row of stools
sunset's clone long gone
the sigh we share with strangers

Sixty Two

< >

missing that high five
with an old buddy
—nothing in common anymore

< >

it's been a tough week
repeat-repeat-repeat
a pint and provisions from the kitchen

< >

miserable days in the city
the squat of all those grays
cardboard cardboard cardboard

Pig State Love Songs

< >

the lovely waitress approaches
Jamaican jerk?
hey, i've been called worse...

< >

wallet, check
hat, tip
hey blue eyes your raincoat

< >

bottoms of the ninths
curves you can't handle
the closest ones hurt the most

Sixty Four

< >

some things won't ever change
outside the pub
sip & sip go the puddles...

< >

weekends
from whim to whim
convenience store atms

< >

for example with tinfoil
hopping in a box
Mr. Pickle is leaving now

Pig State Love Songs

< >

coming down bessemer
could it get any worsemer
cops with body cams

< >

cruising in the far right lane
state-owned vehicles
foot on the break

Sixty Six

< >

gray skies at the edge
relax
you still have a chance

< >

among the darkness
a streak of lightning!
interrupting a madman

< >

progress on the ultimatum
the disappearing line
from A to B

Pig State Love Songs

< >

expectation
covers the imagination
with the first snowflake

< >

amnesia
between excuses
there must be my worst enemy

< >

last night's alcohol
washing the mirror
it's not budda, only the devil

< >

a p.m. of bad dreams
pouring coffee
while blinking

< >

midnight lamplight
lest some forget
hard storms make decent company

< >

how many jokes do you know
please, tell me, robot
tell me

Pig State Love Songs

< >

bleak of the night
crying in the tub
there's never enough

< >

the object of desire
unattainable
these rehabilitation themes

< >

quivering birds
on the porch rails
wait for the cat's breakfast

Seventy

< >

flopping around the house
no new messages.
—surprise!

< >

how sluggish any day could go
lingering things above
—unmoving

< >

what dogs do
when it pours from dawn to dusk
likewise

Pig State Love Songs

< >

sitting? staying?
tamed by impulses
at times i fret like an animal

< >

in a free man's land
stuck.
protein from a can

< >

in a free man's land
stuck.
from a can, protein

< >

fat snowflakes
defy gravity
grabbed fast into silent company

< >

tracing a face and idle hands
voyeuristically:
the clock doesn't blink

< >

window on the snow
chilling by kindling
not thinking about nothing...

Pig State Love Songs

< >

offerings from a couch
man minus dream
bowing to the TV—scream

< >

smiley-faced balloons
hauling a mirror
this new personality

< >

in a revolution year
you know whose been true—
pig state *i love you*

Pig State Love Songs

Pig State Love Songs

www.ingramcontent.com/pod-product-compliance
Lightning Source LLC
Chambersburg PA
CBHW031455040426
42444CB00007B/1117